T0148528

Good Food for
Good Health

Good Food for Good Health

MALINI RAJOO

iUniverse LLC
Bloomington

GOOD FOOD FOR GOOD HEALTH

iUniverse books may be ordered through booksellers or by contacting:

iUniverse LLC
1663 Liberty Drive
Bloomington, IN 47403
www.iuniverse.com
1-800-Authors (1-800-288-4677)

ISBN: 978-1-4917-3020-1 (sc)
ISBN: 978-1-4917-3021-8 (hc)
ISBN: 978-1-4917-3022-5 (e)

Library of Congress Control Number: 2014905959

Printed in the United States of America.

iUniverse rev. date: 04/08/2014

Contents

Special Thanks to My Husband

I would like to thank my husband for his encouragement and love in writing this book. He and I took all of the cookery pictures presented in this cookbook. We love travelling and exploring the foods of different countries, their unique spices, and the various cultural styles of cooking. These experiences provide us with a lot of inspiration and widen our horizons toward cooking healthy, creative, and good food.

11/10/2012

This picture was taken in Paris at Les Ombres restaurant; the chefs there were fantastic and the food was absolutely scrumptious.

Acknowledgement

I would like to take this opportunity to dedicate this book to our beautiful and beloved parents who were Rajoo Kuppu and Rohini Maikel (my parents), and my husband's dad, William Edward Farquhar (my dad-in-law), whose souls have left us from this world and gone to heaven. They have shared their cooking knowledge with us and we will be eternally grateful from the bottom of hearts for imparting the artful knowledge of cooking, good values, and culture to us. We will always feel their presence and spiritual guidance. We pray to God for our parents' souls to rest in peace and to give us their blessings and guide us spiritually.

We are going to try our very best to help people lead a healthier lifestyle by cooking and eating healthy food using the recipes in this book.

Introduction

With this book, we would like to share with you our recipes and our parents' secret recipes. I cooked most of the recipes on the spot and the pictures were taken immediately.

This cookbook was written and all the dishes prepared with genuine concern for the health of all human beings in the world. For all of the dishes, we only used extra virgin olive oil and natural and healthy authentic Indian spices and other western spices as the recipes are a fusion of all sorts of foods from different cultures.

The recipes are divided into vegetarian and non-vegetarian food categories.

Also, I would like to share a few words of wisdom:

"Good food is for good health," and

"Cooking is good for our souls, bodies, and minds."

I have also used the picture of Lord Ganesha as he adds symbolic meaning and blessings to this cookbook. By receiving his grace, we receive the grace of all and he removes all obstacles and enables our endeavors to succeed.

Vegetarian Recipes

Vegetarian Curry with Stir-Fried Cabbage

Vegetarian curry and stir-fried cabbage can be served with basmati rice and papadams as condiments. Papadams are a thin, crisp, disc-shaped Indian food made from lentils, black gram, chickpeas, and rice flour. This dish is very simple to cook and is filled with nutrients.

As with most of the dishes where rice is involved, I will be using basmati rice because it is gluten free and low in fat, and it tastes sensational.

Ingredients required for the vegetarian curry:
- ½ a cup of Orange lentils
- 3 Potatoes cut into quarters
- 3 Carrots cut into smaller pieces
- 2 Tomatoes cut into quarters
- 1 white Onions sliced thinly, 1 teaspoon of ginger, and garlic
- 2 tablespoons of Extra virgin olive oil
- 2 teaspoons of Sea salt or iodized salt
- 1 teaspoon of black mustard seeds, half a teaspoon of crushed red chili flakes, and turmeric powder;
- 6 Curry leaves

Method for cooking vegetarian curry:

➢ Preparation of ingredients: 10 to 15 minutes
➢ Cooking time: 30 minutes

1. Wash 1/2 cup of orange lentils and soak in a bowl of water with 1/2 teaspoon of turmeric powder, a pinch of salt, and 1 teaspoon of extra virgin olive oil.
2. Heat the curry pot over a medium flame on the stovetop and pour in 2 tablespoons of extra virgin olive oil. Reduce the heat to low and add minced garlic and ginger, sliced onions, curry leaves, black mustard seeds, 1/2 teaspoon of crushed chili flakes, and turmeric powder, and stir-fry all the ingredients until golden brown.
3. Add all the cut potatoes, carrots, and tomatoes to the pot and stir-fry for another 10 minutes.
4. Then, pour the orange lentils that have been soaking in water with turmeric and salt to the curry pot and stir all the ingredients together.
5. Add another 1/2 teaspoon of turmeric and 1 teaspoon of salt and pour in 1 liter of water. Stir the curry and let it boil for 10 minutes on a medium heat. Please do not let the curry evaporate; add another ½ liter of water and allow the curry to boil for another 20 minutes or until all the ingredients are cooked.

Stir-Fried Cabbage

Ingredients required for stir-fried cabbage:
- ➤ 1 cabbage
- ➤ 1/2 teaspoon of turmeric powder
- ➤ 1 teaspoon of sea salt
- ➤ 1 white onion, sliced thinly
- ➤ 1 teaspoon each of garlic and ginger
- ➤ 1 teaspoon of black mustard seeds

Method for cooking stir-fried cabbage:
- ➤ Preparation of ingredients: 10 minutes
- ➤ Cooking time: 10 minutes

1. Wash the cabbage and cut it finely into thin slices.
2. Heat the frying pan on the stove over a medium flame and pour 1 tablespoon of extra virgin olive oil into the hot frying pan, tilting the pan to spread the oil.
3. When the oil is medium hot, add the onions, garlic, and ginger and stir-fry until golden brown.
4. Add the turmeric powder and black mustard seeds; stir-fry for another 2 minutes.
5. Then, add the cabbage to the pan, stir-fry it and add the salt.

6. Pour 1/2 cup of water into the pan and stir-fry the cabbage again.
7. Let it cook for 10 minutes, and then it is ready to be served.

🖎 **Note**: *Using garlic, ginger, and turmeric in the diet will help to immunize the body against infection and prevent a person from catching the flu. Ginger is good for the digestion, too.*

Ingredients required for basmati rice:

➤ 1 cup of basmati rice per person
➤ A pinch of saffron
➤ 1 teaspoon of extra virgin olive oil
➤ A pinch of sea salt;

🖎 **Note:** *Saffron is an expensive spice that is made from the saffron crocus flower. It is also used as an herbal supplement that is claimed to be helpful for a variety of conditions, including depression, asthma, and insomnia.*

Method for cooking basmati rice with a rice cooker:

➤ Preparation of ingredients: 10 minutes
➤ Cooking time: 15 minutes

1. Add 1 cup of rice for each person.
2. Wash the rice, and put it in the rice cooker. If you are making two cups of rice, add water until it reaches mark two in the rice cooker.
3. Add the salt, extra virgin olive oil for a smooth texture, and the saffron to the rice.
4. Press the rice cooker button to cook the rice; normally, the rice will be cooked within 15 minutes.

Method for cooking basmati rice on the stove top:

1. If you do not have a rice cooker, cook the rice in a pot on the stove. Add 1 cup of rice and 1 cup of water for each person.

2. Then, add the salt, extra virgin olive oil for a smooth texture, and the saffron to the rice, and cook for about 15 minutes. Please stir the rice after 15 minutes to check the texture, as it should be nice and fluffy.

Method for cooking papadams:

➤ Preparation of ingredients: No preparation required
➤ Cooking time: 30 to 40 seconds

1. You can buy mini papadams at the supermarket and microwave them in a deep bowl for 30 to 40 seconds.
2. Microwaving the papadams eliminates the need to fry them.
3. Normally, the papadams are best prepared using a deep bowl.

Gluten-Free Vegetarian Stir-Fried Noodles
(Serves 6)

A vegetarian stir-fried noodle dish is a healthy option and a very light dish to eat it for dinner. I add chilies and capsicums to the noodles as they have many health benefits. Chilies are an excellent source of Vitamins A, B, C, and E with minerals like molybdenum, manganese, folate, potassium, thiamine, and copper. Chili also contains seven times more vitamin C than an orange.

> ✎ **Note:** *For those who are unable to consume chili, you can just add onions, garlic, and ginger.*

Chillies were introduced to India in 1498, and it have been included in Ayurvedic medicines and used as tonic to ward off many diseases. Chilies are good for slimming as they help to burn calories more easily. Chilies also stimulate the appetite, help to clear the lungs, and aid the digestive system. The shitake mushrooms, which I use in this recipe, help to lower cholesterol.

Ingredients required for stir-fried noodles:
  - ➤ 1 packet of rice noodles
  - ➤ 3 tablespoons of extra virgin olive oil
  - ➤ 1 white onion, thinly sliced
  - ➤ 1 teaspoon each of ginger and garlic
  - ➤ 2 Spring onions, sliced thinly
  - ➤ 1 small packet of bean sprouts

➢ 1 teaspoon of chili paste or 1 green or red chili
➢ 2 tablespoons of low salt black soy sauce
➢ 2 tablespoons of vegetarian oyster sauce
➢ 3 eggs
➢ 1 packet of dried shitake mushrooms
➢ 1 packet of organic firm bean tofu
➢ 1 red capsicum, sliced thinly
➢ 1/2 teaspoon of turmeric powder
➢ 2 teaspoons of iodized salt or sea salt
➢ 1/2 teaspoon of chili powder.
➢ Mixed vegetables (you can get pre-cut mixed vegetables, such as sliced cabbage and carrots, in the supermarket, which saves preparation time)

Method for cooking vegetarian noodles:
➢ Preparation of ingredients: 10 to 15 minutes
➢ Cooking time: 20 to 30 minutes

1. Boil some hot water and pour some into a large bowl to soak the rice noodles until soft for 5 minutes. After 5 minutes, drain the water as you do not want the noodles to become too soft.
2. Pour the other half of the water into a small bowl to soak the dried shitake mushrooms for another 5 minutes.
3. Prepare all the ingredients and heat the stir-fry wok for 5 minutes. Pour 2 tablespoons of extra virgin olive oil into the wok.
4. Add the onions and stir-fry until golden brown. Then, add the minced garlic and ginger to the wok and stir-fry this.
5. Add the chili paste or a finely chopped red or green chili, and break in 3 eggs and scramble.
6. Remove all of the scramble eggs from the wok and arrange on a plate.
7. Season the tofu with 1/2 teaspoon of turmeric powder, 2 teaspoons of iodized salt or sea salt, and 1/2 teaspoon of chili powder. Stir-fry the tofu until it is crispy and cooked.
8. Remove the tofu and leave it in a separate bowl.
9. Then add another tablespoon of extra virgin olive oil to the hot pan and add the rest of the onions and stir-fry for 1 minute.

10. Drain the shitake mushrooms and add to the pan along with the vegetarian oyster sauce; stir-fry for 5 minutes with ½ a teaspoon of garlic and ginger.

11. Add the thinly sliced red capsicum and the drained rice noodles little-by-little to the wok and stir fry quite well; then, add 1 tablespoon of low salt soy sauce.

12. Remember to add the rice noodles to the wok little-by-little so that the ingredients are nicely mixed together. If the noodles are too dry, add 1/2 cup of water and more soy sauce, plus 1 tablespoon of tomato sauce if desired, to get the right taste.

13. Then, add the scramble eggs to the noodles and stir-fry again for 5 minutes until all the ingredients are mixed properly.

14. Now, it is ready to serve.

15. Any leftover noodles can be stored in glass or plastic containers and refrigerated. Just warm-up and enjoy for lunch or dinner the next day.

Stir-Fried Eggplant, Bok Choy, Shitake Mushrooms, and Tofu served with Basmati Rice
(Serves 4)

> ➤ Preparation of ingredients: 10 minutes
> ➤ Cooking time: 20 minutes

This is a delicious dish that can be prepared quickly. The dish consists of eggplant, which has a lot of minerals and vitamins, such as B1-6, and shitake mushrooms, which boost the body's immune system and contain iron, which helps to prevent cancer cells according to doctors' research. Bok Choy is very low in calories, contains vitamin C, and has other minerals beneficial for the body. Finally, the tofu is a high source of protein, calcium, and vitamin E.

Ingredients required for stir-fried eggplant, bok choy, shitake mushrooms, and tofu:
> ➤ 3 tablespoons of extra virgin olive oil
> ➤ 1 white onion, sliced into quarters
> ➤ 1 teaspoon each of ginger and garlic_
> ➤ 1 white onion thinly sliced
> ➤ 1 teaspoon each of turmeric powder and sea salt or iodized salt
> ➤ 1 tablespoon of vegetarian soy sauce
> ➤ Pinch of ground black pepper

- ➢ 1 firm organic piece of tofu cut into small cubes and ½ tablespoon of iodized or seasalt to season the tofu
- ➢ 3 bunch of Bok choy sliced into halves
- ➢ 1 purple eggplant cut into small pieces
- ➢ 1 cup of dried shitake mushrooms;

Method for cooking stir-fried vegetables with tofu:

1. Boil some hot water and pour some into a bowl to soften the shitake mushrooms for 5 to 10 minutes and drained the water.
2. Prepare all the ingredients and heat the wok for 5 minutes. Pour 2 tablespoons of the extra virgin olive oil into the wok.
3. Cut and marinate the tofu with the turmeric powder, 1 teaspoon of sea salt or iodized salt, and a pinch of ground black pepper. Use a good quality non-stick pan so that you do not have to use so much oil.
4. Stir-fry the marinated tofu until it is slightly crispy; then remove it and put it on a separate plate.
5. Then, add 1 tablespoons of extra virgin olive oil to the wok; heat the oil and add the minced garlic and ginger and the cut onions to the hot oil.
6. Stir-fry until golden brown and add the vegetarian oyster sauce.
7. Add the shitake mushrooms and the cut eggplant to the wok, and stir-fry it until it is mixed well with the vegetarian oyster sauce.
8. Add the bok choy to the wok and stir-fry with 1 teaspoon each of minced garlic and ginger and 1 teaspoon of vegetarian oyster sauce.
9. At the end, add the crispy tofu to the dish and gently stir-fry with the rest of the ingredients.
10. Finally, stir-fry the eggplant, bok choy, shitake mushrooms, and tofu and serve with some basmati rice.
11. This is a very simple and healthy dish to prepare.

Gluten-Free Vegetarian Penne with Kalamata Olives
(Serves 4-5)

Vegetarian gluten-free penne is a healthy dish for dinner and it is very convenient to cook. I have added olives to the dish as they are a good source of anti-oxidants and are loaded with vitamins. Pine nuts are a good source of fiber, manganese, protein, and other vitamins.

Ingredients for vegetarian gluten-free penne
- One bag of gluten-free penne
- 1 cup of sliced mushrooms
- Extra virgin olive oil
- 1 teaspoon of iodized salt and ground black pepper
- Fresh oregano and oregano flakes
- 1 white onion, thinly sliced
- 1 teaspoon of minced ginger and garlic
- 1 small cup of sliced kalamata or black olives
- 1 small bottle of pesto sauce bought from the supermarket

Method for cooking vegetarian penne:
- Preparation of ingredients: 10 minutes
- Cooking time: 20 minutes

1. Boil some hot water and pour all the penne into the boiling water; add 1 tablespoon of extra virgin olive oil and add a pinch of salt and oregano.

2. Boil the penne for 8 to 10 minutes until it is cooked and then drain the water and place the penne in a large bowl.
3. Then, add 1 tablespoon of extra virgin olive oil, a sprinkling of oregano, and a pinch of salt to the drained penne. Stir the penne well until it is well-coated with the oil so that it cannot stick together.
4. Heat your pot, pour two tablespoons of extra virgin olive oil, and stir-fry the garlic, ginger, and onion until golden brown.
5. Then, add all the sliced mushrooms and stir-fry with the garlic, ginger, and onion; add the packet of pine nuts to the pot and stir-fry all of the ingredients.
6. Add the pesto sauce and kalamata olives and allow this to cook for 2 to 3 minutes.
7. Finally, add the penne and toss this very well until all of the ingredients are mixed together.
8. It is now ready to be served and you can keep the left over pasta for the next day's lunch.

Vegetarian Fried Rice

Vegetarian fried rice is a delicious dish when cooked with the right kind of vegetables. I have added cabbage, capsicum, shitake mushrooms, white onion, eggs, and tofu, which is a good source of protein.

Ingredients required for the vegetarian rice:

- ➢ 2 cups of basmati rice
- ➢ A pinch of saffron
- ➢ Extra virgin olive oil
- ➢ Iodized salt
- ➢ 1 white onion, thinly sliced
- ➢ 1 green chili, thinly sliced
- ➢ 1 teaspoon of chili paste
- ➢ 1 firm organic tofu
- ➢ 1 cup of shitake mushrooms (dried shitake mushroom need to be soaked in hot water for 5 minutes to soften)
- ➢ 2 tablespoons of vegetarian oyster sauce
- ➢ 1 teaspoon each of ginger and garlic
- ➢ 2 table spoon of low salt soy sauce to stir fry the rice
- ➢ 1 teaspoon of turmeric powder
- ➢ 1/2 cabbage, thinly sliced;
- ➢ 1 teaspoon of paprika powder
- ➢ 3 eggs
- ➢ 1 small cucumber for side salad.

Method for cooking vegetarian fried rice:

- ➢ Preparation of ingredients: 10 to 15 minutes
- ➢ Cooking time: 20 to 30 minutes

1. Cook the basmati rice with one tablespoon of extra virgin olive oil and a pinch of iodized salt and saffron.

2. While the rice is cooking, cut the firm tofu into small pieces and marinate with turmeric, iodized salt, and a teaspoon of paprika.
3. Stir-fry the tofu with extra virgin olive oil until it is crispy and golden brown; then, heat up a medium-sized wok or an electric wok, pour in some extra virgin olive oil and allow it to get hot.
4. Add the onion and stir-fry until golden brown.
5. Drain the water out from the shitake mushroom and start adding the garlic, ginger, and shitake mushrooms.
6. Add the cut green chili to the oil and stir-fry it.
7. Add two tablespoons of vegetarian oyster sauce to cook the shitake mushrooms.
8. Add the chili paste, break the eggs, and scramble.
9. Then add the cabbage and the crispy tofu to the wok to stir-fry.
10. Add the cooked basmati rice and stir-fry with the rest of the ingredients.
11. Then add the low salt black soy sauce to the rice and stir fry until nicely cooked.
12. The rice is then ready to be served with the cut cucumber slices.

Indian Roti Prata (Indian Pancake) with French Beans and Served with Vegetarian Curry

Roti prata is a pan-fried Indian pancake and is a very light dinner. Today, there is no need to cook the Indian roti from scratch. You can buy the dough at the supermarket and pan-fry it with olive oil. Serve with vegetarian curry (recipe above) and stir-fried French beans. If you want to do the roti from scratch, the recipe is as follows.

This dish is very popular in Asian countries, such as Singapore and Malaysia.

Ingredients required for Indian roti prata
- 250 grams of gluten free flour or normal whole meal flour
- 1 teaspoon of iodized salt
- 1/2 teaspoon of brown sugar
- 1/2 cup of warm water
- 5 teaspoons melted low cholesterol butter
- 1/2 cup of low-fat milk;
- 3-6 tablespoons of extra virgin olive oil

Method for Cooking Indian Roti Prata:-
- Preparation of ingredients: 10 to 15 minutes to prepare the dough and 5 to 6 to hours for the dough to rise, if you are rushing for time you can buy the pre-pared flat indian pancakes at a supermarket or an indian grocery store.

> ➤ Cooking time: 2 minutes to pan-fry the roti until it is golden brown.

1. Sift the flour in a large bowl, add the low cholesterol butter, and mix well until it becomes crumbly.
2. Slowly pour in the low-fat milk and mix well.
3. Knead the dough without adding extra flour until it can be pulled away from the bowl and you can make small balls of dough. This should take from 10 to 15 minutes.
4. Then cut the dough into 12 pieces and roll each piece into a soft ball.
5. Massage each ball with extra virgin olive oil and flatten; placed the flattened dough on a tray and cover with a clean wet cloth. Allow the dough to rest for 5 to 6 hours to rise.
6. Heat a flat pan for 2 minutes and pour in 2 tablespoons of extra virgin olive oil.
7. When the oil is at the right temperature, flatten the soft dough balls and stretch them with your hands into a reasonably sized circle and put them in the pan.
8. Cook until they become golden brown, fluffy, and crispy.
9. Serve with vegetarian curry and French beans.
10. This dish can be enjoyed at breakfast, lunch, or dinner.
11. For breakfast, you can break an egg on the roti prata and cook it in the pan; then, eat it as it is with a nice cup of coffee.

Stir-Fried French Beans with Scramble Eggs

According to history French beans were originated in South and Central America ages ago and they are healthy and low in calories. They contain excellent source of minerals and vitamins.

Ingredients required for stir-fried French beans with or without eggs

- ➢ French beans
- ➢ 1 white onion
- ➢ 3 eggs
- ➢ 3-6 tablespoons of extra virgin olive oil
- ➢ Iodized salt
- ➢ 1 teaspoon each of garlic and ginger
- ➢ 1/2 teaspoon of black mustard seeds
- ➢ 1/2 teaspoon of turmeric powder

Method for cooking French beans:

- ➢ Preparation of ingredients: 10 to 15 minutes
- ➢ Cooking time: 10 to 15 minutes

1. Heat up the wok and pour in some extra virgin cooking oil.
2. Cut the white onion into slices and stir-fry it with the garlic and ginger.
3. Then, add the black mustard seeds and turmeric powder and stir-fry with all the other ingredients.

4. Break the eggs, add a pinch of salt and black pepper, and scramble.
5. Add the cut French beans to the wok and stir-fry.
6. Serve with the roti or basmati rice and vegetarian curry.

Egg Curry

Egg curry is a high-protein dish and is easy to prepare. I have added a lot of cherry tomatoes to this dish, which are a rich source of vitamin C.

Ingredients required for egg curry and stir-fried cabbage

- 6 hard-boiled eggs
- 1 teaspoon of minced garlic and ginger
- 2 tablespoons of curry powder
- 1 teaspoon of garam masala
- 1/2 teaspoon of turmeric powder
- 1/2 tablespoon of iodized salt
- 3-6 tablespoons of extra virgin olive oil
- 3 tomatoes, sliced into quarters
- 1 white onion, sliced
- 1 container of low salt tomato paste which can be bought from the supermarket
- Cut potatoes, peas, and carrots can also be added to the curry

Method for cooking egg curry:

- Preparation of ingredients: 10 to 15 minutes
- Cooking time: 20 to 30 minutes

1. Boil the eggs in a pot of water in their shells.
2. When hard-boiled, cool the eggs in some cold water.
3. Then, peel the eggs and place them on a plate.
4. Heat the curry pot and pour the extra virgin olive oil into the pot.
5. Add the sliced onion and stir-fry until golden brown; add the minced garlic and ginger, curry powder, garam masala, turmeric powder, and 1 teaspoon of salt.
6. Stir-fry until you can smell the aroma of the spices.
7. Add another tablespoon of oil if necessary, as you cannot let the spices burn.
8. Add the tub of tomato paste and all of the other ingredients, such as tomatoes, potatoes, peas, and carrots if you like.
9. Pour in 2 cups of water and allow this to cook for 15 minutes.
10. Taste one of the potatoes to check whether it is properly cooked.
11. Stir the curry well, ensuring that it is the right thickness and not too watery.
12. Then, add all of the hard-boiled eggs to the curry and let this cook for another 10 minutes.
13. When the curry is done, taste it to check whether it has enough salt.
14. Serve with some basmati rice, stir-fried cabbage (see recipe), and papadams.

Vegetarian Biryani with Cauliflower, Peas, and Potatoes

My husband, Chris, and I cooked and wrote the vegetarian biryani recipe together and the side dish is cauliflower and potatoes. You can serve the vegetarian biryani with some papadams and mango pickles.

 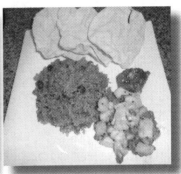

Ingredients required for vegetarian biryani
- ➤ 3 cups of basmati rice, washed
- ➤ Patak's mild or hot biryani paste or another brand of paste
- ➤ 1 teaspoon each of minced garlic and ginger
- ➤ 1 white onion, thinly sliced
- ➤ 1 teaspoon of iodized salt
- ➤ 1 teaspoon of garam masala
- ➤ 1/2 teaspoon of turmeric powder
- ➤ A pinch of saffron soaked in hot water for color and taste
- ➤ 3-6 tablespoons of extra virgin olive oil
- ➤ 6 cardamoms, 2 cinnamon sticks, and 6 cloves
- ➤ Broccoli, carrots, and green baby peas
- ➤ Salted cashew nuts and raisins; however, if you are allergic to nuts, omit the cashew nuts

Method for cooking vegetarian biryani:
- ➤ Preparation of ingredients: 10 to 15 minutes
- ➤ Cooking time: 45 minutes to 1hour

1. Prepare all the ingredients for cooking, such as slicing the onion and cutting the carrots into small slices.
2. Chop the broccoli in bite-size pieces and rinse in a colander.
3. Heat the pot and pour in some olive oil; stir-fry the onions, garlic, and ginger for 2 minutes.
4. Add the garam masala, turmeric powder, cardamom, cinnamon sticks, and cloves and stir-fry for 2 minutes until you can smell the aroma of all the spices mixed together.
5. Then, add all the vegetables, peas, raisins, and cashew nuts and stir-fry.
6. Add the Patak's biryani paste to the pot.
7. Add 1 teaspoon of iodized salt.
8. Stir all the ingredients for about 3 minutes and add the washed basmati rice.
9. Boil some water and add some saffron to the boiled water; the color will become orange-red.
10. Add the saffron to the rice and add 2 cups of water to the pot.
11. Cover the pot and bake the rice in the oven at 200 degrees Celsius (392 Fahrenheit) for about 40 minutes to 1 hour.
12. After half an hour, take the pot out of the oven to check the rice; stir it with a spoon or fork and test the texture.
13. Put the pot of biryani back into the oven and bake for another 15 minutes.
14. Take the rice out again and check by stirring with a fork; reduce the oven to 150 degrees Celsius (302 Fahrenheit) and bake for another 15 minutes.

Cauliflower, Peas, and Potatoes

Ingredients required:
- ➢ 1 cauliflower, washed and cut into bite-size pieces
- ➢ 1 cup of green baby peas
- ➢ 1 teaspoon each of minced garlic and ginger
- ➢ 1 white onion, thinly sliced
- ➢ 1 teaspoon of black mustard seeds
- ➢ 2 teaspoons of iodized salt
- ➢ 1 teaspoon of garam masala
- ➢ 1/2 teaspoon of turmeric powder
- ➢ 2 peeled potatoes cut into quarters and boiled in water for about 10 minutes until medium-soft

Method for cooking the cauliflower:
- ➢ Preparation of ingredients: 10 minutes
- ➢ Cooking time: 10 to 15 minutes

1. Heat the pot and pour in some olive oil; stir-fry the onions, garlic, and ginger for 2 minutes.
2. Add the black mustard seeds, garam masala, turmeric powder, and stir-fry it for 2 minutes until you can smell the aroma of all the spices mixed together.

3. Then, add the boiled potatoes, cut cauliflower, and peas and stir-fry until the spices are mixed together with all the ingredients.
4. Add 1/2 cup of water and 1 teaspoon of iodized salt and stir well.
5. Taste the vegetables to check if there is enough salt; add another teaspoon of salt if necessary.
6. Stir the vegetables and cook for about 5 to 10 minutes until nicely tender.
7. Serve with side condiments, such as papadams and Indian mango pickles, as shown in the above picture.

Note: The easiest way to cook papadams is to microwave 4 or 5 of them in a deep bowl for about 30 to 40 seconds and also look for the instructions to microwave papadams that is always written behind the back of the box or packet.

Vegetarian Burger with Quinoa and Red Beans
(Serves 6)

This vegetarian burger is a very healthy and delicious dish for dinner. Quinoa is a super food, rich in protein, iron, fiber, magnesium, and lysine. Lysine is essential for tissue growth and repair.

I have also added red beans, which are very healthy for the body, beneficial for the heart, and contribute to increased vitality. According to medical research, red beans contain vitamin C, vitamin K, vitamin B1, vitamin B2, vitamin B6, folic acid, calcium, iron, magnesium, phosphorus, potassium, zinc, copper, selenium, omega-3 and omega-6 fatty acids, fiber, and protein.

Ingredients required for the vegetarian burger:
> 1/2 cup of quinoa;
> 1 can of organic red kidney beans
> 1 teaspoon each of minced garlic and ginger
> 1 teaspoon of cumin powder
> 1/2 teaspoon of cinnamon powder, turmeric, Mexican chili powder, and garam masala
> 1 egg
> 1 cup of gluten-free bread crumbs
> 1/2 tablespoon of iodized salt
> 3-6 tablespoons of extra virgin olive oil
> 1 white onion, thinly sliced (Tip: after cutting the onions, rinse in water to get rid of the milk)
> 1 red pepper, thinly diced
> Multi-grain buns or gluten-free buns

Method for cooking vegetarian burger:

➤ Preparation of ingredients: 10 to 15 minutes
➤ Cooking time: 30 minutes

1. Wash the quinoa and boil it in hot water for about 15 minutes with a teaspoon of olive oil and a pinch of iodized salt.
2. Pour the red kidney beans into a large bowl and mash it roughly.
3. Break an egg into the bowl, stir well and add salt and pepper to taste.
4. Add the sliced onion and diced red peppers.
5. Add the minced garlic and ginger, turmeric powder, cinnamon, Mexican chili powder, and 1 teaspoon of iodized salt.
6. Add 1 tablespoon of lemon and herb breadcrumbs or use plain breadcrumbs if preferred.
7. Stir the mixture well and form into patties as shown above.
8. Pan-fry or bake the burgers in the oven for 30 minutes at 325 Fahrenheit (170 degrees celsius); keep an eye on the patties so they do not burn. I normally put baking paper sprayed with olive oil on the tray so that the patties do not stick. I spray some olive oil on the patties, as well.
9. While the burgers are cooking, prepare some cucumber and tomato slices to use as a garnish or salad.
10. Then, ten minutes before the burger is cooked, caramelize the onion with oyster sauce or Worcestershire sauce, or simply add salt and pepper to it.
11. When the patties are done, place them on the multi-grain buns with low-fat cheese slices, cucumber and tomato, and top with the caramelized onions.
12. You can serve six delicious burger patties for six people and have a healthy dinner with your family and kids.

Mushroom and Capsicum Quesadillas with Corn

Quesadillas are very healthy and simple to cook and make a good meal for kids and the whole family.

Ingredients required for mushroom and capsicum quesadillas and baked corn

- ➢ 1 capsicum
- ➢ 1 spring onion and some chives, thinly sliced
- ➢ 1/2 packet of rocket spinach
- ➢ 1 cup of mushrooms
- ➢ 1 cup of low-fat shredded cheese
- ➢ 1 small jar of sliced kalamata or black olives
- ➢ 1 small jar of sliced jalapenos
- ➢ 1 onion, finely diced
- ➢ 6 corn on the cob, halved, as the side dish

Method for Cooking Mushroom and Capsicum Quesadillas and corn: -

- ➢ Preparation of ingredients: 10 minutes
- ➢ Cooking time: 10 to 15 minutes

1. Rinse, drain, and dry the rocket spinach.
2. Cook the mushrooms in olive oil and add iodized salt and pepper.

3. Preheat the oven to 325 degrees Fahrenheit (175 degrees Celsius); sprinkle 1/2 cup of low-fat shredded cheese on one side of each tortilla.

4. Place two tortillas cheese side up on baking sheets, and bake for 5 minutes or until the cheese is melted.

5. Sprinkle the olives, jalapenos, capsicum, cooked mushroom, rocket and some shredded cheese on the tortilla and cover with another tortilla.

6. Put the covered tortillas in the oven for about 10 minutes until cooked and crispy.

7. After 10 minutes, turn the tortillas over and return to the oven for another 5 to 10 minutes until crispy. This is to ensure that both sides of the tortillas are crispy as the bottom can be a little moist.

8. While the tortillas are cooking in the oven, boil the six halved corn on the cob with some olive oil and a pinch of salt.

9. When the tortillas are done, cut each quesadilla into four wedges and serve with the corn.

Spinach and Ricotta Pastry with Salad and Flat Barbequed Mushrooms

Spinach has an abundance of vitamins A, C, B2, B6, E, K, magnesium, folate (iron), calcium, and potassium. It is also a great source of protein, phosphorus, zinc, fiber, copper, and has good amounts of selenium, niacin, and omega-3 fatty acids.

It prevents inflammatory diseases such as arthritis; osteoporosis, migraine headaches, and asthma, due to its anti-inflammatory properties. Scientific research shows that eating green leafy vegetables slows the age-related decline in brain function.

Ingredients required for spinach and ricotta pastry:
- ➢ 100 grams low-fat ricotta cheese
- ➢ 150 grams baby spinach
- ➢ 1 lime
- ➢ 1/2 white onion, thinly sliced
- ➢ 1/2 teaspoon sweet smoked paprika
- ➢ 1 chili
- ➢ 1 teaspoon of iodized salt and pepper
- ➢ 1/2 teaspoon each of minced garlic and ginger
- ➢ Fresh basil or flakes
- ➢ 1 tablespoon of olive oil
- ➢ 6 large sheets of filo pastry sprayed with olive oil and brushed with egg

Ingredients for salad
- ➤ 3 colors of capsicum, red, green, and yellow
- ➤ Assorted lettuce leaves of various colors

Ingredients for salad dressing
- ➤ Dijon mustard
- ➤ 1 tablespoon of honey
- ➤ A pinch of iodized salt
- ➤ 1 tablespoon of Olive oil
- ➤ Juice of 1 lime

Method for cooking spinach and ricotta:
- ➤ Preparation of ingredients: 10 to 15 minutes
- ➤ Cooking time: 20 to 30 minutes

1. Oil the non-stick pan and lay the filo pastry sheets brushed with egg and olive oil on it.
2. Blend all the ingredients listed above for the spinach and ricotta and season to taste.
3. Pour the thick mixture into the pan, lay some filo pastry over it, and fold nicely. Brush the top layer with olive oil and poke a few small holes through the top with a fork or knife. This is so the pastry will be crispy and not too moist.
4. Then, brush the top with egg so it will be nice and shiny.
5. Bake in the oven at 150 degrees Celsius (300 degrees Fahrenheit) for 20 minutes.

Method for making salad and dressing:
1. Cut all the capsicums nicely and make the salad dressing.
2. Wash the lettuce and drain the water.
3. For salad dressing, mix Dijon mustard, olive oil, lime juice, honey, a pinch of salt and black pepper and mix well.
4. Dress the salad right at the end when the meal is ready.

Flat Barbequed Mushrooms

Ingredients required for barbequed mushrooms
- ➢ 6 flat mushrooms
- ➢ 1 tablespoon of olive oil
- ➢ 1 teaspoon of iodized salt
- ➢ 1 diced green and red chilies
- ➢ ½ a cup of Low-fat shredded mozzarella cheese
- ➢ Half white onion diced and parsley

Method for cooking flat barbequed mushrooms:
- ➢ Preparation of ingredients: 10 to 15 minutes
- ➢ Cooking time: 15 to 20 minutes

1. Wash the mushrooms and pat dry it with a paper towel.
2. Lay the baking paper on the baking tray and spray it with olive oil.
3. Marinate the mushrooms with olive oil, salt, and pepper.
4. Keep some diced chili and parsley to sprinkle right at the end on the mushrooms after sprinkling the mozzarella cheese.
5. Lay the mushrooms on the baking tray upward and fill the mushrooms with diced chili, onions, and parsley.

6. Lastly, sprinkle them with the shredded low-fat mozzarella cheese.
7. Then, right at the end, sprinkle a bit of the diced green and red chilies and parsley.
8. Spray the top part of the mushrooms with olive oil and put in the oven to bake at 150 degrees Celsius (300 degrees Fahrenheit) for about 15 to 20 minutes.
9. Keep an eye on the mushrooms so they do not burn.
10. Serve the spinach ricotta pastry, mushrooms, and the dressed salad for dinner.
11. Bon appetite☺

Vegetarian Gluten-Free Nachos

Vegetarian nachos are simple to cook for either a meal or snack. If you are in the mood for a snack or light dinner, this is a good choice. I have used all healthy ingredients, such as red beans, avocado, tomato salsa, etc. Vegetarian nachos are low in fat and the red beans are good for our health. Avocado contains good fats and is good for the brain with omega-3 fatty acids, vitamins A, C, D, E, and K, and the B vitamins (thiamine, riboflavin, niacin, pantothenic acid, biotin, vitamin B-6, vitamin B-12, and folate) as well as potassium.

Ingredients required for vegetarian nachos:
- ➤ 1 bottle mild tomato, onion, and salsa sauce
- ➤ 1 spring onion, thinly sliced
- ➤ 1 small bottle of sliced kalamata or black olives
- ➤ 1/2 jar of jalapenos
- ➤ 1 can Mexican red beans
- ➤ 1 packet organic, low salt and gluten-free nacho corn chips
- ➤ 1 packet of low-fat shredded cheddar
- ➤ 1 avocado, halved, stone removed, finely chopped
- ➤ 1 fresh lime cut into slices
- ➤ 1 tub of low-fat sour cream, to serve.

Method for cooking vegetarian nachos:
➤ Preparation of ingredients: 10 to 15 minutes
➤ Cooking time: 15 to 20 minutes

1. Preheat oven to 150 degrees Celsius (300 degrees Fahrenheit).
2. Lay non-stick baking paper on the baking tray and spread the gluten-free corn chips.
3. Add the drained beans and spread the jar of tomato, onion, and bean salsa nicely.
4. Sprinkle on the kalamata olives, jalapenos, and the red kidney beans.
5. Sprinkle the low-fat shredded cheese on top of the ingredients.
6. Then add the thinly sliced spring onions on top.
7. Bake in the preheated oven for 15 to 20 minutes at 150 degrees Celsius (300 degrees Fahrenheit) until the cheese is melted.
8. Then, top with sour cream and the sliced avocado.
9. Garnish with some chopped coriander or spring onions.
10. Place the sliced fresh lime on the side of the plate and to squeeze on the vegetarian nachos for a nice snack.
11. You can even have this for dinner, as it is healthy and light.

Seafood

Black Pepper Crabs with Bok Choy and Shitake Mushrooms

This recipe consists of three dishes:
- Black pepper crabs
- Bok choy and shitake mushrooms
- Served with steamed rice

Ingredients required for black pepper crabs:
- Six blue manna (swimmer) crabs, cleaned and cut into halves
- Garlic and ginger
- Ground black pepper
- Oyster sauce
- Olive oil
- Sesame oil
- Gluten-free soy sauce
- 1 teaspoon of Mexican chili powder
- Honey
- Chopped Coriander.

Ingredients for stir-fried bok choy with shitake mushrooms:
- Bok choy
- Garlic and ginger
- Dried shitake mushrooms
- Oyster sauce
- Sesame oil and olive oil

Method for cooking black pepper crabs:

> Preparation of ingredients: 10 to 15 minutes
> Cooking time: 20 to 30 minutes

1. Cook the steamed rice before cooking the crabs and the bok choy and shitake mushrooms.
2. Clean the crabs and cut into halves.
3. In a wok, stir-fry the crabs with oil and iodized salt and black pepper until the shells become orange-red.
4. Take out the crabs and set them aside on a plate.
5. Grind a small packet of black pepper and set aside.
6. Clean the wok and pour some olive oil into it.
7. Add 1 teaspoon each of minced garlic and ginger and stir-fry.
8. Add the ground black pepper, 2 tablespoons of oyster sauce, 2 tablespoons of sesame oil, 1 tablespoon of gluten-free soy sauce, 1 teaspoon of Mexican chili powder, and 1 tablespoon of honey.
9. Add 1 cup of water and mix the sauce for about 5 minutes.
10. Then, add the stir-fried crabs to the wok and mix well with the sauce for about 5 to 10 minutes.
11. Add the chopped coriander and stir-fry the crabs again.
12. Garnish with some coriander after the crabs are cooked.

Method for cooking bok choy and shitake mushrooms:

> Preparation of ingredients: 10 minutes
> Cooking time: 10 to 15 minutes

1. Rinse the bok choy and cut off the bottom stems.
2. Put the shitake mushrooms in a bowl and boil some water.
3. Pour the boiled water into the bowl and soak the shitake mushrooms for about 5 minutes and drain the water after 5 minutes.
4. Heat the pan and pour in some olive oil.
5. Add 1 teaspoon each of minced garlic and ginger and stir-fry.
6. Add the shitake mushrooms and add them to the garlic and ginger; stir-fry with oyster sauce for 5 minutes until cooked and nicely browned.
7. Then, add the bok choy and stir-fry for 5 minutes.
8. When ready, serve the black pepper crabs and bok choy with the steamed rice.

Tandoori Salmon with Potato Patties and Broccolini

This recipe consists of three dishes:
- Tandoori salmon
- Potato patties
- Broccolini

Ingredients required for the tandoori salmon:
- ➤ Six Salmon fish cutlets
- ➤ 1 lemon, sliced in halves to squeeze on the salmon
- ➤ Extra virgin olive oil
- ➤ 1/2 teaspoon of turmeric
- ➤ 1 teaspoon of Iodized salt
- ➤ Half a teaspoon of cracked black pepper
- ➤ 1 teaspoon each of minced garlic and ginger
- ➤ Tandoori paste from any well-known brand, such as Patak's

Method for cooking tandoori salmon:
- ➤ Preparation of ingredients: 10 minutes
- ➤ Cooking time: 15 minutes

1. Marinate the salmon with turmeric, iodized salt, pepper, lemon, garlic, and ginger.

2. Then generously spread tandoori paste on the salmon cutlet and marinate for 10 minutes.

3. Then, spray extra virgin olive oil on the salmon cutlets and place on a baking tray and bake for 15 minutes.

Potato Patties

- ➢ Preparation of ingredients: 10 minutes
- ➢ Cooking time: 30 to 40 minutes

Ingredients required for the potato patties:
- ➢ 4 boiled and peeled potatoes
- ➢ Extra virgin olive oil
- ➢ 1 tablespoon of iodized salt
- ➢ ½ teaspoon of turmeric
- ➢ ½ teaspoon of garam masala
- ➢ 1 cup of green peas
- ➢ ½ Cracked black pepper
- ➢ 1 teaspoon each of minced garlic and ginger paste
- ➢ 2 spring onions thinly sliced and cut 1 green or red chilies with seeds removed

Method for cooking potato patties:
1. Mash the potatoes into a medium texture.
2. Combine all of the ingredients with the mashed potatoes and mix until blended.
3. Then form the potato mixture into small patties and place on a baking tray lined with baking paper.
4. Spray some extra virgin olive oil on the patties.
5. Bake the potato patties for about 30 to 40 minutes at 150 degrees Celsius.
6. The picture below shows how the potato patties should look when ready: -

Ingredients required for broccolini:

➢ Preparation of ingredients: 5 minutes
➢ Cooking time: 1 minute

- Broccolini
- 1 tablespoon of extra virgin olive oil;
- 1/2 tablespoon of iodized salt

Method for cooking broccolini:

1. Boil the broccolini for about 1 minute.
2. Add the salt and the olive oil while it is boiling.
3. Then, after 1 minute, drain all the water and serve with the tandoori salmon and potato patties.

Coconut Rice with Anchovies and Hard-Boiled Chili Paste Eggs

This recipe consists of six dishes:
- Coconut rice with green peas
- Stir-fried tofu
- Anchovies
- Hard-boiled eggs
- Cooked chili paste with or without anchovies (available from Asian shops)
- Tomato and cucumber salad

Ingredients for coconut rice with green peas:
- ➤ 3 to 5 cups of Basmati rice depends on the guests
- ➤ 1 cup of green peas
- ➤ ½ teaspoon of iodized salt and 1 teaspoon of olive oil for the rice
- ➤ Light coconut milk
- ➤ Approximately 6 hard-boiled eggs, depending on the number of people
- ➤ Dried anchovies
- ➤ Cooked chili paste with or without anchovies
- ➤ 1 organic firm tofu

> ➤ 1 teaspoon of paprika
> ➤ 1 teaspoon of turmeric
> ➤ 2 ripe tomatoes and a cucumber for the salad

Method for cooking coconut rice with green peas:
> ➤ Preparation of ingredients: 10 minutes
> ➤ Cooking time: 30 to 40 minutes

1. Wash 3 or 5 cups of basmati rice depending on the guests or family members and put in the rice cooker.
2. Pour in one small can of light coconut milk, ½ teaspoon of iodized salt, and 1 teaspoon of olive oil.
3. Wash 1 cup of green peas and add them to the rice cooker.
4. Add 2 to 3 cups of water and stir the rice before it begins cooking.
5. Start the rice cooker to cook the rice.
6. When the rice is almost cooked, stir it and cover the rice cooker to finish cooking.
7. Cut the organic tofu into cubes and rinse it.
8. Season the tofu with 1/2 teaspoon each of paprika and turmeric, 1 teaspoon of iodized salt, and 1 tablespoon of olive oil.
9. Stir-fry the tofu until crispy.
10. Wash the anchovies and dry them before stir-frying. You won't need much oil to stir-fry the anchovies. Please use a non-stick pan or a stone dine pan for good health.
11. Anchovies only take 5 to 10 minutes to become crispy so lower the flame to medium so they don't burn.
12. Boil 3 to 6 eggs, depending on the number of people.
13. Cool the hard-boiled eggs for 5 minutes, peel, and cut into halves.
14. When done, put 4 tablespoons of cooked chili paste in a pan and heat on a low to medium flame. Put a bit of chili paste in the middle of each egg yolk to serve as shown in the picture.
15. Slice the tomatoes and cucumber in circular forms to decorate the plate for the salad.

16. Garnish the cooked chili with dried onions and serve with the coconut rice and all the other ingredients as shown in the picture above.

17. This meal is quick and easy and it is nice to have it for dinner with your family and friends with an authentic taste.

Fish Curry with Okra, Kale, and Baked Fish

Fish curry is a very scrumptious and healthy dish. I have taken the opportunity to add tomatoes, eggplant, okra, also known as ladies' fingers, and potatoes, which are all very nutritious.

Okra has several health benefits that, according to research, include improving eyesight, preventing anemia, helping with weight loss, fighting diabetes, and boosting the immune system. Eggplant contains calcium, iron, vitamin K, bioflavonoids, and other essential minerals, is low in fat, is a good source of fiber, provides heart benefits, and regular consumption will help prevent blot clots. Tomatoes are rich in vitamin C, prevent DNA damage and cancer, and have other health benefits.

According to nutritionists' studies, potatoes do not only have carbohydrates, but are also a good source of fiber. They also help reduce inflammation since they contain vitamin C, calcium, protein, B vitamins, amino acids, and omega-3 and other fatty acids. They are also good for brain function as they help balance glucose and oxygen levels. The best ways to cook potatoes are boiled, baked, air-fried, or cooked in a curry.

For the vegetable, I have used kale, which has lots of vitamins such as A and K, is low in calories, high in calcium and iron, and has lots of anti-oxidants.

Finally, I have used cod or mackerel since they are low in calories, high in protein, and a great source of omega-3 fatty acids. They also provide a lot of energy, and are good sources of vitamins B6, B12, and vitamin D, which reduce inflammation among other health benefits.

This recipe consists of the following dishes:
- Cod or mackerel cutlets
- Tomatoes
- Okra (ladies' fingers); if this vegetable is unavailable, it can be omitted
- Potatoes
- Eggplant (Brinjal)

- Kale
- Marinated fish cutlets baked in the oven

Ingredients for the fish curry:

- ➤ 6 cod or mackerel (if cod is unavailable) cutlets
- ➤ 1 tablespoon of salt
- ➤ 1 teaspoon each of turmeric powder, chili, iodized salt, and pepper for the marinate
- ➤ 3 tablespoons of olive oil
- ➤ 1 teaspoon fenugreek seeds
- ➤ 1 medium piece of ginger, peeled and chopped
- ➤ 4 cloves garlic, chopped
- ➤ 1 large white onion, sliced thinly
- ➤ 6 tablespoons fish curry powder mixed with 1 cup of water to form a paste
- ➤ 3 tomatoes, chopped
- ➤ 2 large potatoes, diced into quarters
- ➤ 5 ladies' fingers (okra), chopped
- ➤ 2 brinjals (eggplants), chopped
- ➤ Salt and pepper
- ➤ Chopped fresh coriander to garnish and to add to the curry while cooking.

Ingredients for the kale:

- ➢ 1 bunch of healthy kale, washed and cut into smaller pieces
- ➢ 1 teaspoon each of minced garlic and ginger
- ➢ 1/2 white onion, diced
- ➢ 1/2 teaspoon of turmeric
- ➢ 3 tablespoons olive oil

Method for cooking kale:

- ➢ Preparation of ingredients: 10 minutes
- ➢ Cooking time: 10 minutes

1. Cut the kale into smaller pieces and rinse in a colander.
2. Heat the pan, pour in the olive oil, and add the chopped onions.
3. Stir-fry the onions until golden brown, add the garlic and ginger and 1/2 teaspoon each of turmeric and iodized salt.
4. Add the kale and stir-fry until it shrinks in size; then taste for salt.

Ingredients for baking the fish before cooking the fish curry:

- ➢ 6 cod or mackerel (if cod is unavailable) cutlets
- ➢ 1 tablespoon of turmeric powder, 1 teaspoon of chili, 1 teaspoon of iodized salt, half a teaspoon of pepper, and 3 tablespoons of olive oil;
- ➢ Marinate the fish with the above ingredients and leave for 10 minutes.

Method for baking the fish:

- ➢ Preparation of ingredients: 10 minutes
- ➢ Cooking time: 15 minutes

1. Line a baking tray with baking paper and spray some olive oil on it.
2. Place the marinated fish on the tray and bake in the oven at 200 degrees Celsius (390 Fahrenheit) for about 15 minutes or until the fish is crispy.

3. While the curry is cooking, keep an eye on the fish so that it doesn't burn.
4. When the curry is almost done add some of the baked fish to the curry and simmer for 10 minutes. Use the rest of the baked fish for a side dish as shown in the picture.

Method for Cooking Fish Curry:

➢ Preparation of ingredients: 15 minutes
➢ Cooking time: 30 to 45 minutes

1. Wash the fish and pat dry.
2. Marinate it with olive oil, salt, pepper, turmeric, chili powder, and olive oil all over and set aside for 10 minutes.
3. Put it on a baking tray lined with baking paper, and bake the fish at 200 degrees Celsius (390 Fahrenheit) for 20 minutes or until crispy.
4. When the fish is nicely baked and crispy, remove it from the oven.
5. In a large cooking pot, heat the olive oil over medium heat until hot.
6. Add the fenugreek seeds and cook until the seeds start to pop, about 1 minute.
7. Add the ginger and garlic and stir-fry this.
8. Stir-fry the onions and cook for another minute.
9. Add 3 tablespoons of fish curry powder to warm water to dissolve it; then, reduce the heat to low and add the curry paste.
10. Stir-fry until the paste is fragrant and starts to darken, and the oil starts to ooze from the paste, about 2 to 3 minutes.
11. Be careful not to burn the curry paste, as it has to stir-fry at the right temperature.
12. Add 4 cups of water and bring to a boil.
13. Add the potatoes.
14. Season to taste with iodized salt and pepper; if it is too spicy, add 1 teaspoon of brown sugar.
15. Bring to a gentle boil, adding more water if the gravy is getting too thick, and ensure that the potatoes are tender.

16. Then, add the ladies' fingers (okra), brinjal (eggplant), and tomatoes and allow this to cook for 10 minutes.

17. Once the fish is baked, keep four fish cutlets for a side dish and add the rest of the baked fish to the curry along with a bit of the chopped fresh coriander. I have baked the fish so that the flesh of the fish won't fall apart, but the flavor of the fish curry will still seep into the flesh of the fish.

18. Then, cover the pot and simmer for 15 minutes. This is so the curry will soak into the fish and the flavors of the gravy and fish will blend.

19. Please do not overcook the fish cutlets as they have already been baked in the oven.

20. Taste the fish curry for salt and ensure all the ingredients are cooked right.

21. When the curry is cooked, turn off the heat and leave it for 10 minutes for the flavors to mingle.

22. Then, garnish the curry with fresh chopped coriander and serve immediately with naan bread, crispy roti prata (Indian savory pancake), or with some basmati rice.

✦ **Note:** *The remaining fish curry can be kept in the fridge for the next day's dinner, and usually, the fish curry tastes delicious the next day. However, please do not leave the fish curry in the fridge for more than two days.*

Spaghetti (Gluten-Free) with Prawns and Cherry Tomatoes

Gluten-free spaghetti with chili prawns is a simple dish to cook, too.

- 9 king prawns, peeled and cleaned
- Gluten-free spaghetti
- 1 small jar of kalamata or black olives
- 1 tub of cherry tomatoes, sliced into halves
- 1 teaspoon of iodized salt or sea salt
- Cracked black pepper
- 1 teaspoon of minced garlic and ginger
- Chili flakes
- Sliced lemons for garnishing.

Method for cooking gluten-free spaghetti with king prawn:

➢ Preparation of ingredients: 10 minutes
➢ Cooking time: 15 to 20 minutes

1. Boil your spaghetti in hot water for 6 to 9 minutes and season it with olive oil, salt, and pepper.
2. Cut one or two of the noodles with a fork to see if they are cooked properly and be sure not to overcook them.
3. Drain the noodles, pour them into a large bowl, and season with olive oil so they do not stick together.
4. Wash and clean the prawns and stir-fry in a big wok with garlic, ginger, and a teaspoon each of salt and pepper.

5. Once the prawns are cooked nicely, add the cherry tomatoes, kalamata olives, and sliced onions and stir-fry again.
6. Add the gluten-free spaghetti to the wok, toss, and stir-fry.
7. Add more olive oil if necessary, and also add a bit of the chili flakes and a pinch of iodized salt.
8. Stir the noodles and the other ingredients for 10 to 15 minutes until the noodles are mixed properly with the rest of the ingredients.
9. Serve the gluten-free prawn spaghetti for dinner for your friends and family.

Gluten-Free Healthy Baking Recipes

For all my baking recipes, I have only used gluten-free flour and healthy ingredients.

Gluten-Free Blueberry Muffins with Chia Seeds

These blueberry muffins can be eaten for breakfast or an afternoon tea break. Chia seeds are an excellent source of calcium, magnesium, iron, zinc, boron, niacin, essential amino acids, protein, and vitamins B, D, and E. They have more digestible protein, antioxidants, omega-3, calcium, and iron than beans, soy, or peas, and aid in reducing inflammation in the digestive tract.

Ingredients required for gluten-free blueberry muffins:
- 1 cup of blueberries
- 250 grams gluten-free flour
- 2 tablespoons of low cholesterol butter
- 1 tablespoon of vanilla extract
- 1 teaspoon of cinnamon powder
- 1 teaspoon of baking powder
- 2 tablespoons of chia seeds
- 3 eggs
- 1 cup of low-fat milk
- 1 cup of brown sugar

Method for baking blueberry muffins:
- Preparation of ingredients: 10 minutes
- Cooking time: 20 to 25 minutes

1. Beat the eggs until fluffy; then, add the vanilla extract and brown sugar and beat for about 5 minutes.
2. Mix the butter, chia seeds, and milk gently with the gluten-free flour until the mixture is the right texture.

3. Then, add the blueberries and mix gently.
4. Line a muffin tray with muffin cups and spray them with extra virgin olive oil.
5. Fill each muffin cup halfway with the muffin mixture so the muffins have room to rise.
6. Then, spray some oil on the mixture as this will give the muffins a shiny texture.
7. Preheat the oven to 150 degrees Celsius (300 Fahrenheit).
8. Bake the muffins for 20 to 25 minutes and check the muffins after 15 minutes as they may be cooked.
9. You can also test by inserting a toothpick into the center and seeing if it comes out clean.
10. If the mixture does not stick to the fork when it is removed, the muffins are baked properly. If you still see a bit of mixture, put the muffins back in the oven for another 5 minutes.
11. When the muffins are ready, cool for 10 minutes and serve the muffins to your family and friends for breakfast or teatime with coffee or a nice green tea.

Healthy Carrot and Walnut Gluten-Free Cake

For this cake, I have used all healthy and low-fat ingredients.

Carrots are a good source of fiber and have lots of health benefits, such as improving eyesight, benefitting the skin, and helping to prevent cancer.

Walnuts are packed with omega-3, boost heart health, and reduce stress levels. I have also used raisins in this recipe, which, according to medical research, aid digestion, increase energy, protect the eyes, and treat anemia.

It is surprising what cinnamon can do. According to scientific research, it regulates blood sugar, reduces cholesterol, acts as a natural food preservative, and reduces the pain linked to arthritis. Cinnamon also helps to prevent Alzheimer's disease and has other health benefits.

Ingredients required for carrot and walnut cake:
- 2 medium carrots, peeled and grated
- 1/2 cup chopped walnuts
- 2 small packets of raisins
- 3 eggs
- 1/2 cup of brown sugar or 2 tablespoons of manuka or other natural honey, as the natural sweetness will also come from the raisins and you do not want the cake to be too sweet
- 2 tablespoons of low cholesterol butter
- 1/2 cup of extra virgin olive oil
- 1/2 teaspoon vanilla essence

> ➤ 200 g cup of gluten-free self-rising flour for a 2-inch cake (If you want the cake to be higher, you can bake two 2-inch cakes and make two bowls of cream to put between the layers
> ➤ 1 teaspoon of baking powder
> ➤ 1 teaspoon of cinnamon powder

Ingredients required for carrot cake frosting:

> ➤ 2 tablespoons of low cholesterol butter
> ➤ 2 egg whites
> ➤ 1 teaspoon vanilla extract
> ➤ 1/2 cup pure icing sugar

Method for making the frosting:

> ➤ Preparation of ingredients: 10 minutes
> ➤ Cooking time: 15 minutes

1. Put the egg whites in a large bowl and beat with an electric mixer until fluffy and white.
2. Then, add two tablespoons of low cholesterol butter, vanilla, and 1/2 cup of icing sugar and beat with the electric mixer until light and fluffy.
3. Add 3 tablespoons low-fat milk or light cream, vanilla essence, and beat until smooth.
4. Beat in more milk until desired spreading consistency is reached and the frosting is spreadable.
5. Ensure that the cake is cool before you apply the frost.
6. Makes about two cups of frosting, enough to frost the top layer of the cake.
7. Then, to make it presentable, arrange some walnuts on top and sprinkle on some cinnamon powder as shown in the picture above.

Method for cooking carrot and walnut cake:

> ➤ Preparation of ingredients: 10 minutes
> ➤ Cooking time: 30 minutes

1. Grate 2 medium carrots and place in a bowl.
2. Break 3 eggs into a blender and add 1/2 cup of brown sugar, 2 tablespoons of low cholesterol butter, and blend until smooth.
3. Take 1 cup of gluten-free self-rising flour and mix well with the egg and brown sugar mixture.
4. Then, add ½ cup of extra virgin olive oil, 1 teaspoon of baking powder; ½ teaspoon of mixed spice, ½ teaspoon of cinnamon powder, and ½ teaspoon of vanilla essence.
5. Blend all together in the blender.
6. Then, add ½ cup of walnuts and the grated carrot to the cake mixture and blend well for 5 minutes.
7. Preheat the oven to 150 degrees Celsius (390 Fahrenheit).
8. Pour the cake mixture into a well-greased ring tin or a tin lined with baking paper and sprayed with some olive oil to prevent sticking.
9. Sprinkle some crushed walnuts on top of the cake for decoration before you bake the cake in the oven.
10. Bake the cake for 30 minutes at 150 degrees Celsius (390 Fahrenheit) and keep an eye on it to prevent burning.
11. Test the cake by using a fork or knife to poke the top surface of the cake.
12. When the fork is removed, if the cake mixture does not stick to it, the cake is done.
13. Apply the cake frost and decorate the cake with some walnuts and dust with cinnamon powder.
14. It is advisable to cool the cake for 10 minutes before serving to your family and friends. Serve with a cup of green tea or mint and lavender tea.

Banana Bread with Walnuts, Chia Seeds, and Jarrah Honey

Banana bread is a great food that you can have for your breakfast or for a tea break. To make it even healthier, you can add chia seeds and vegetable or olive oil instead of butter. If you want to use butter, you can use low-fat butter or olive oil butter.

Ingredients required for banana bread with chia seeds:

➤ 250 g of gluten-free bread flour
➤ 1 teaspoon of baking powder
➤ 3 ripe bananas
➤ 2 eggs
➤ 3 tablespoons of Jarrah honey or other brand or one cup of brown sugar
➤ 1 tablespoon of cinnamon
➤ 1 tablespoon of chia seeds
➤ 1 tablespoon of vanilla extract
➤ 3 cups of vegetable oil or olive oil
➤ ½ a cup of walnuts

Method for baking banana bread:

➤ Preparation of ingredients: 15 minutes
➤ Cooking time: 30 minutes

1. Preheat oven to 175 degrees Celsius (350 degrees Fahrenheit).
2. Grease and flour two 8 x 3 inch loaf pans.

3. Whisk together the flour, baking powder, and baking soda.

4. Mash the bananas, eggs, honey, cinnamon, salt, and baking soda.

5. Stir in the melted butter and vanilla extract, and then fold in the flour mixture until a batter forms and no dry lumps remain.

6. Pour into the prepared loaf pans and bake in preheated oven for about 45 minutes.

7. You can test the mixture by inserting a knife into the center of the bread until it comes out clean.

8. Cool the banana bread for 10 minutes; then remove from the pan and cut and serve the slices to your family and friends for breakfast or coffee break.

Gluten-Free Apple and Cinnamon Pie

This apple pie is made from gluten-free flour, apples, walnuts, and cinnamon and is a good dessert for after dinner.

Ingredients required for apple pie pastry:

> 250 g of gluten-free flour
> 3 tablespoons of low-fat butter
> 1/2 cup of raw sugar
> 1 teaspoon of cinnamon
> 1 teaspoon of vanilla essence
> 2 free range eggs
> 1/2 cup low-fat warm milk
> Olive oil to grease the pan

Ingredients required for apple pie filling:

> 6 large Pink Lady or Granny Smith apples
> 1 teaspoon of cinnamon
> 1 teaspoon of vanilla essence
> 2 tablespoons of brown sugar (as apples already have natural sweetness)
> Crushed walnuts
> 2 cups of water

Method for cooking healthy apple pie pastry:

> Preparation of ingredients: 15 minutes
> Cooking time: 30 minutes

1. Beat the 2 eggs; then add 1/2 cup of raw fine sugar and 3 tablespoons of butter and mix with an electric beater.
2. Then, add 2 drops of vanilla essence, 1 teaspoon of cinnamon powder, warm milk, and the flour slowly while mixing with a wooden spoon.
3. After all the flour is mixed properly, beat well with an electric beater.
4. Roll the dough with extra flour until all of the mixture sticks together; leave it in a bowl for 30 minutes.

Method for cooking healthy apple filling:

➢ Preparation of ingredients: 15 minutes
➢ Cooking time: 30 minutes

1. Peel 6 Pink Lady or Granny Smith apples and dice the apples into quarters.
2. Boil 1/2 pot of water and add the apples to the boiling water with two tablespoons of raw sugar.
3. Let it boil for 15 minutes until the apples are caramelized.
4. Cool the mixture for about 15 minutes.
5. Grease the apple pie pan and place the pastry in the pan.
6. Then slowly add the apple filling to the pan and crumble some walnuts on top.
7. Decorate the top part of the apple pie with nice strands of pastry in a crisscross manner and bake the apple pie for 30 minutes.
8. Cool the apple pie for 15 to 20 minutes.
9. Serve the apple pie with fat-free custard sprinkled with cinnamon and a cup of tea.
10. Enjoy!

Gluten-Free Bread with Chia and Sesame Seeds

This is gluten-free bread baked with chia seeds that have natural goodness. To bake the bread in a simpler way, I bought the whole meal gluten-free flour bread mix and added my own ingredients to it, such as sesame seeds and chia seeds.

Ingredients required for gluten-free bread:
> ➤ 450 grams of organic gluten-free whole meal bread flour
> ➤ 550 ml of warm water
> ➤ 1 teaspoon dried yeast
> ➤ 30 ml of vegetable oil
> ➤ 2 tablespoons of chia seeds
> ➤ 1 teaspoon iodized salt

Method for baking gluten-free bread:
> ➤ Preparation of ingredients: 15 minutes
> ➤ Cooking time: 30 minutes

1. Preheat the oven to 200 degrees Celsius (390 Fahrenheit) and spray olive oil on a non-stick baking tray.
2. Combine the gluten-free flour, yeast, 2 tablespoons of chia seeds, and iodized salt in a large bowl.
3. Add all the ingredients above and use a wooden spoon to stir the mixture until well combined; then, using your hands, bring the dough together in the bowl.
4. Turn onto a lightly floured surface and knead for 10 minutes or until the dough is smooth and elastic.

5. Place the dough on the baking tray and level it to the size of a bread loaf; sprinkle the top with sesame seeds and spray the top with some olive oil.
6. Cover with a damp tea towel and set aside in a warm place to rise for 30 to 45 minutes or until the dough has almost doubled in size.
7. Then bake the bread at 200 degrees Celsius (390 Fahrenheit) for 30 minutes.
8. When the bread is baked, take it out of the oven and leave it to rest and cool for 20 minutes.
9. You can then serve this for breakfast with blueberry jam.